W9-BDM-593

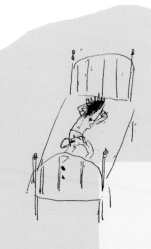

i.d

Stuff That Happens to Define Us

Kate Scowen   Peter Mitchell

annick press
toronto + new york + vancouver

We acknowledge the support of the Canada Council for the Arts, the Ontario Arts Council, and the Government of Canada through the Book Publishing Industry Development Program (BPIDP) for our publishing activities.

 ONTARIO ARTS COUNCIL
CONSEIL DES ARTS DE L'ONTARIO

Cataloging in Publication

Scowen, Kate
    i.d. : stuff that happens to define us / Kate Scowen ; illustrated by Peter Mitchell.

ISBN 978-1-55451-224-9 (pbk.).—ISBN 978-1-55451-225-6 (bound)

    1. Life change events—Juvenile literature. 2. Identity (Psychology)—Juvenile literature. I. Mitchell, Peter II. Title.

BF723.I56S36 2010   j155.4'182   C2009-906165-1

Distributed in Canada by:
Firefly Books Ltd.
66 Leek Crescent
Richmond Hill, ON
L4B 1H1

Published in the U.S.A. by:
Annick Press (U.S.) Ltd.
Distributed in the U.S.A. by:
Firefly Books (U.S.) Inc.
P.O. Box 1338
Ellicott Station
Buffalo, NY 14205

Printed in China.

Visit us at: www.annickpress.com
Visit Peter Mitchell at: www.petermitchell.net

FOR SYDNEY, HATLEY, AND QUINN—
THE BEST PARTS OF MY STORY.
—K.S.

FOR MY SARA, JACKSON, AND ISABEL.
—P.M.

CONTENTS

INTRODUCTION

Everybody has a story, no matter where they come from or where they have ended up. My hope is that by reading other people's stories, you'll start to think about your own.

Thinking about **your** story is a big part of getting to know yourself, and becoming comfortable with who you are. With this knowledge and comfort firmly in hand, you'll be better equipped to face the many challenges and successes that are headed your way.

There will be many moments in your life when you ask yourself "Who am I?" If you're dealing with hardship, bad family situations, or internal struggles it can be especially hard to see past the tough times. But life isn't just about the here and now. You still have a lot of life ahead of you, and that means there are a lot of opportunities for making positive change.

The stories in this book are about that kind of positive change. I asked a few people I know who have remarkable stories to share them with me. I also sent out a call for stories through emails to networks of friends and colleagues, and through flyers that I posted at community and youth centers. People who sent in stories told me how much they really liked thinking about their identities. Many felt that retelling their stories was a healthy thing for them; it kind of reaffirmed their identities and reminded them of who they are. I wish we could have included more of the stories people sent in but we only had room for 12.

A few of the stories are moments in time, single events that shifted people's identities completely, like a punch in the face (**Punched**), being kidnapped (**Drive**), getting into a fight (**The Fight**), or being deceived (**Broken-hearted**). Others take place over a longer period of time, showing how identity can evolve slowly as we try to define ourselves apart from the burdens that confine us, like living in chaos (**Mom**) or a family's expectations (**Stuck**). Some stories are about the identities people create for themselves as protection from the things they can't control in their lives, like a family breakup (**Orphan Boy**), destructive parents (**Freefall**), or violence (**Reconciliation**). Others still show how our identities can be shaped by the ways we try to fit in to meet people's expectations of us, as we deal with things like body image (**Big Girl**), immigration (**Exotic**), and sexuality (**Playing House**).

All of the stories in this book are about the ways we accept and define ourselves throughout our lives, and how, for better or worse, they shape who we become. In many ways, each of these stories is a great example of how we can become the master of our own identity. They show us that what defines us in youth doesn't have to confine us forever.

This realization came at different times and through different means in each story. All of these people were willing to question their identities, own their stories, and be open to change—in some cases, they demanded it. The Q&A after each story tells you a bit more about how each person got there.

What really brought this book to life were Peter's illustrations. After I edited the stories, he took over, interpreting them with his own vision. He didn't know anything about the people behind the stories but he produced 12 beautifully realized pieces. I hope that you can find yourself in one of these stories, or bits of yourself in a few.

And I hope that recognition helps you to start thinking about who you are within the context of your own story. Learning and accepting your story, and your role within it, can help you to make the positive changes that will keep you resilient and strong throughout your life.

Note: Not all stories are equal—some are so destructive that the process of dealing with them can be overwhelming. If you are dealing with a story like that, get help. Talk to a counselor, a friend, or trusted adult who can help you find the support you need. You can find numbers to Canadian and U.S. hotlines in the Resources section on page 158.

reconciliation

When I was growing up, I witnessed and experienced a lot of violence.

To COPE, I chose to believe that bad things happened for a reason. It was the only way I could reconcile why I would have been subjected to all of these awful things. I believed that every good thing that happened to me happened only because I had suffered so much ~ like a kind of giant balancing act.

Wonder what they did wrong?

People around me were afraid of violence. While other girls were scared of the city at night, I felt free to walk anywhere at any time, because there was really nothing as frightening on the streets as in my home. My comfort with violence became a kind of fearlessness, a kind of bravery.

Finally, when I was **14**, my mother managed to escape her abusive boyfriend.
But my anger and pain didn't go away. I ran away from home, got really into punk rock, and started drinking and doing drugs. At the time it seemed like a good way to release some of my violent energy without actually hurting anybody.

When I was 16, I moved back home and tried to get it together. I had a really close friend who was angry too. He had gotten way too heavy into drugs and had just been released from rehab. Together we tried to stay clean and fumbled for a way to cope without drinking and taking drugs. We had lots of laughs. But then...

... he killed himself.
      I was Devastated.
The belief system that I
had depended on to keep
me sane completely fell
apart. I just couldn't
believe that he died
for a reason or that
something good would
come from it.

I still carry
around an incredible
sadness from all the things
I experienced as a kid.
But I've also accepted that
good and bad things will
happen to me, whether or
not I can find reason in them.
Somehow I've managed to
hold on to my strong
sense of hope.

RECONCILIATION Q&A

HOW DID YOU MANAGE TO MOVE FORWARD AFTER YOUR FRIEND DIED?

I withdrew from my friends; it hurt too much when they died. A few years later there was this new guy at work who decided he wanted to be friends with me. He would kind of follow me around on breaks and just talk to me, no matter how surly or silent I was. And he would smile and just be consistent in his friendliness.

He kept inviting me for coffee after work and I kept finding excuses not to go. One day he wore me down and I said, "Okay, fine, I'll go!" When we got to the coffee shop there were three of his other friends there. I was so mad; I felt tricked, forced into a social situation. We had a fight about it afterward, but it was the first time since my friend died that I could "feel" that someone wanted to be my friend. His patient and persistent friendship rescued me from the fear and sadness I was feeling. It made me feel hopeful again.

I came to accept that there was not much I could do about the bad things that had happened in my life but that I could actually make good things happen by being open to them. And my friend's consistent, gentle presence is what made it possible for me to get out of that funk. He helped me realize that the risk of loving someone and losing them, the challenge of making a friend, is worth it.

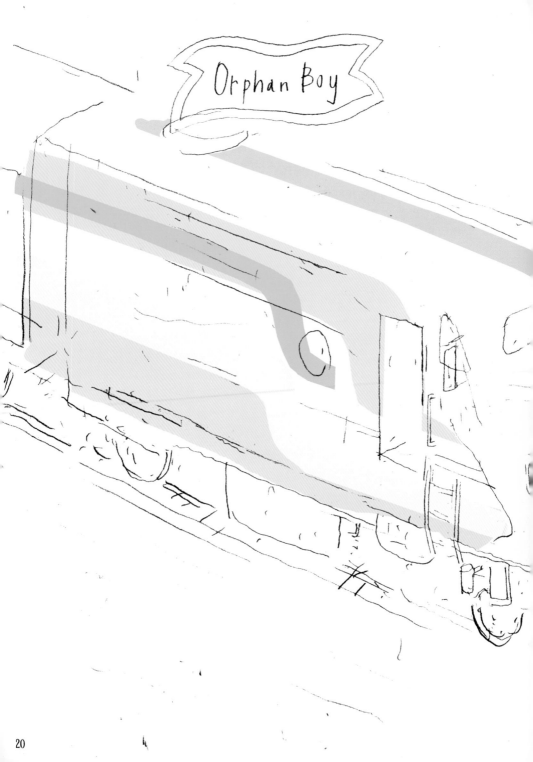

I was 15 and away at boarding school when my housemaster informed me that my parents needed me to take the train home for some kind of family emergency. I had no idea what awaited me.

I must have known my parents were living apart but I don't remember them telling me. My father and I waited in his depressingly **Brown** bachelor apartment for my mother to arrive. She never took off her coat. They told me they were getting a divorce. Dad had been fooling around on her for years.

As my mother got up and left, my dad and I followed her into the hallway. She just wanted to leave but the elevator wouldn't come. She paced, almost panicked. I tried to hug her; I was so worried about how she felt.

After she left, my
father took me to a cocktail
party; he apparently couldn't
miss. He never asked me
how I was feeling; he
acted like nothing had
happened. I walked around
in a fog of shock.

The next day I was put back on a train to boarding school. I never lived with my mother or siblings after that night. I was assigned to my father and I often came home to an empty apartment.

I had trouble at school the next few years. My Grades collapsed. I got into fights with friends and teachers. I basically just stopped caring about the world around me. I had no one to talk to, no one to hear me say how much I had loved being in that great family. I honestly felt Orphaned.

I developed a fantasy life in which my parents and sisters were killed in a car crash while I was away at school. A complete orphan, I strike out on my own and form a wildly successful punk band as I courageously struggle to overcome my terrible loss.

Not as sick as it sounds,
it was a true reflection
of what I felt happened to
me. It was a way of expressing
my feelings while keeping
them to myself because
I was so ashamed of them;
they were too hideous to
share.

The experience made me long for the intimacy and sense of belonging I had lost, but it also caused me to keep people at a distance. Bad combination. I made poor choices about the people I was with; I committed to them without knowing them or giving much of myself in return.

ORPHAN BOY Q&A

WHAT WAS IT ABOUT THAT EXPERIENCE THAT MADE YOU KEEP PEOPLE AT A DISTANCE?

It made me feel worthless, that my feelings were irrelevant and not worthy of anyone's attention. I eventually stopped listening to my own feelings and just felt what people told me to feel.

That was a big mistake on my part. I should have taken responsibility for how I felt. I was angry and I should have said "Fuck them." I should have given my parents hell and not spared them a second of my anger. Instead I kept it bottled up inside.

I still have trouble telling people how I really feel; I keep my distance so I don't have to. It can be hard work to be my friend.

WAS THERE ANYTHING THAT HELPED YOU OVERCOME THIS?

Time, mostly, and experience. It took me a while but I finally found someone who really loves me and gets me, and with whom I feel safe saying what's on my mind or in my heart.

I also have my sisters, who shared my experience in their own ways. We talk about it, acknowledge the craziness of it all, and support each other in dealing with it. Living through a broken marriage together had become an unbreakable bond.

playing house

When I was a little
girl I had a *Best* best
friend and we did absolutely
EVERYthing together. I think
I was really bossy.

As we got a little older we started to play "house". This involved turning the bedroom into a makeshift kitchen. I was always the Daddy and she was always the mammy. This game also involved a certain amount of kissing.

Our game probably should have stopped when we were kids, but it went on for years. We were so wrapped up in each other that we never questioned it.

When I was a
teenager, I discovered
that it was not something
everybody else was doing
and our relationship
really confused me and
stressed me out.
Eventually our
friendship fell apart.

the Mustang

I felt really messed up about it and dated a lot of men, searching for the RIGHT GUY to solve the problem.

It took me a few more years to come to terms with the fact that I was queer. Ultimately, It was that first relationship that helped me realize I was not straight, and never had been.

PLAYING HOUSE Q&A

DID YOU EVER TALK TO YOUR FRIEND ABOUT WHAT WAS GOING ON BETWEEN YOU?

Not really. Somehow we normalized what we were doing to the extent that it didn't seem like behavior that was different or "deviant." We had this really meaningful and satisfying relationship but we also had boyfriends and we were sexually active with them, so we never questioned our "games"; it was just what we did.

WHY DO YOU THINK IT TOOK YOU SO LONG TO COME TO TERMS WITH YOUR SEXUALITY?

I grew up in a confusing household. My parents had lots of gay friends and definitely identified with a gay lifestyle, but they presented themselves as a straight couple. It was like they couldn't acknowledge to themselves or anyone else who they really were. And even though there were lots of gay women around our house, my mom often made negative remarks about the way they looked. I wanted to be pretty and girly and I didn't have a role model for that kind of lesbian. I couldn't identify with any of them. There was really no space for me in that world to question my own sexuality.

Eventually it was the pressure from society, peers, and family that destroyed my relationship with that girl. I was so confused; the societal norms I felt I had to fit into to make me feel safe ultimately made me feel stifled.

After I left home it took me a few more years but I was finally able to come to terms with my sexuality. When I discovered queer theory and queer activism I began finding more and more spaces and people that I felt comfortable with. That's when I found my queer identity.

Broken-hearted

I'm 16 years old ~
Never been kissed.
Decent hair , testosterone, (quite a bit)
Long bad-luck streak with
The ladies. Could be the
the glasses.

And then a **Mixer** is
held between my public school
and the Local "Rich Kid" school,
and this hot rich girl picks me
out of the crowd and asks me
to dance. ALL it takes
is one kiss and I am head
over heels in Love. I don't
eat for **3** days. I feel
possessed by mysterious,
powerful, and warm forces.

I try to stay calm. I do everything I can to build it, work it, and make it last. We spend the next 2 months making out in my father's truck and talking on the phone late into the night.

She's my date for prom and the night is perfect. I take her home, hold her, make out with her awhile, and then walk her to her door.

Driving home I notice she's left her purse in my car and I pace back to return it.

I pull up to her house, which is fairly mansion-like, and she's standing in a shadow on the porch making out with another guy. He's the major jock at her school ~ a real dick too.

They don't even
notice I've driven up
so I toss her bag onto
the yard, Wait until
she looks, then speed
away... into a brakdown.

I drove aimlessly for 2 hours, going from hysterical and weeping to silent and shaking ~ just shattered. For about six months I was a surly, sullen wreck.

I don't know which
emotion was the most valid -
anger, sadness, despair, or
shame - but I had them all.
I felt as intensely bad as
I had felt good when we
were together. For a long
time I struggled to trust
anyone, including myself,
but I did get over it,
eventually.

BROKEN-HEARTED Q&A

AFTER YOU DROVE INTO YOUR BREAKDOWN, HOW DID YOU RECOVER?

It was hard. It was a big blow to my ego because I was on such a high about it. She was the girl everybody wanted and she chose me. I really thought she loved me and I was confused—it didn't make any sense.

So I shut down for a while—not only in terms of how I looked at girls, but also with friends and family. I needed time and distance to work my way back to being open and trusting people.

I threw my hurt and anger into sports, exhausting myself each day so that I wouldn't have to face my own self-criticisms and the questions people were asking. I stopped hanging around with my circle of friends who knew her to avoid talking about what happened. Eventually, I found new friends and built new relationships.

That first cut was deep and it took a long time before I would ever let myself fall that hard again. Eventually I met another girl; we fell in love and it was good. I had my guard up a bit so I would be ready for it when it ended; I wasn't as naïve. That relationship ended mutually, with a sense of respect, which helped me to realize that it's okay to feel love, and to trust it.

Big Girl

I was **18** years **old** the summer before my last year of high school. I had **TONS** of confidence and I was popular at school, but I didn't like my body; I was the "big girl." I figured it would be easier for people if they knew that I knew I had big thighs. So it became **my** thing to publicly critique my own body.

you think those are **big**? **LOOK** at these!

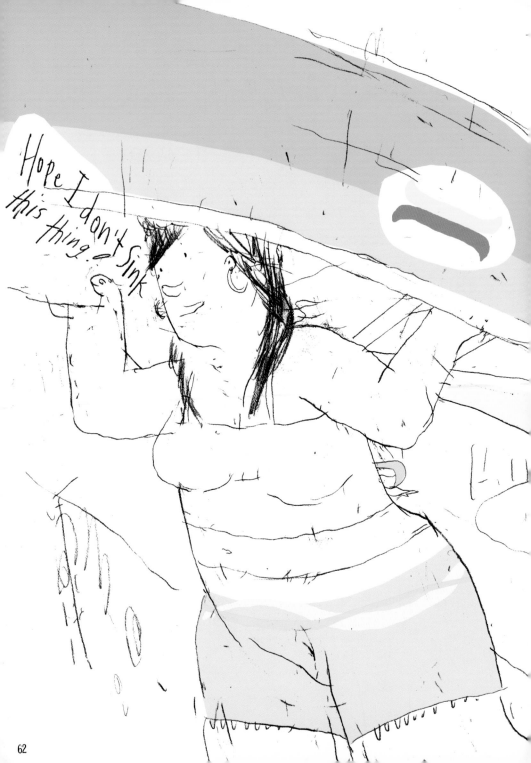

Hope I don't sink this thing.

That summer, I went on a youth Wilderness trip. We kayaked, sailed, rowed, and rock-climbed for 21 days. Three of those days I spent on a SOLO trip, alone in the bush with very (little) food and no books to read. The whole experience was

Great!

maybe I should wear two.

poke
poke

On the Last day of the
trip, the group got together
over the Campfire and had a
talk where everyone got to
hear what everyone else
honestly thought of them after
3 weeks in the Wilderness.

My best friends on the trip were 2 older guys. During the talk each one said to me in his way that he loved many things about me but couldn't tolerate my self-criticisms about my body.

They explained that every time they heard me say how big my thighs were, I became a little less attractive to them. I was embarrassed but I couldn't ignore their honesty.

What was said at
that campfire changed my
outlook toward my body,
and my life in general. From
that point on I accepted
my big thighs as part of
who I am. I stopped
imposing my issues with
them on anyone else.

BIG GIRL Q&A

HOW WERE YOU ABLE TO TURN WHAT WAS SAID AT THAT CAMPFIRE INTO SUCH A BIG PERSONAL CHANGE?

It didn't happen right away but I slowly shifted away from being that person who was always criticizing herself. After that trip I remember hearing girls and women participate in the constant self-critiquing that I was trying to escape. I just knew I didn't want to be like that anymore.

Ultimately, it was my sense of confidence that led the change. A big part of my self-esteem came from my mother. She taught me to focus on the important things in life: family, friends, and school. Never once did she suggest that I was "big" or that I shouldn't eat something because it would make me fat. She was always supportive; in her eyes, I knew enough to make the right decisions, I always looked great, and there was no reason why I couldn't do anything I wanted to do. Those small tokens of trust, respect, and love went a long way.

Leaving home opened me up to more change. I had grown up in a small town and went to university in a big, exciting city. Late nights, wonderful food, new friends, and a great school—I was in heaven. My independence boosted my confidence even more and I stopped worrying about my body; I was having too much fun.

I have always struggled with my weight but I have also learned to accept my body as it is. There have been times when I wished I was thinner, but I've come to realize that a life spent wishing I was someone else wouldn't be much fun, for me or the people around me.

I was 11 when we moved to a new town. My parents were going through a nasty divorce. My mother had full custody but my father used to take us without her permission, and sometimes he wouldn't let us go home.

I remember the sick feeling, the panicked rush to leave, the intensity of my mother's driving, and her chain-smoking with the windows rolled up. I could sense her fear and it scared me.

On the first
day at our new school,
my brother and I were
walking back together after
Lunch. All of a sudden we saw
a car driving backwards down
the street, and it stopped just
ahead of us. It was my Dad.

I've some business in town. Get in and I'll drive you back to school!
Hi! what are you doing here

I Promise, hop in.

Promise you'll take us to school

I knew we had made
a mistake as soon as
we got into the car. My
Dad sped up the street and
pulled a fast U - turn
onto the highway.

My first reaction was sheer anger. I screamed at him. I called him every swear word I knew. But after a few minutes I felt an innate sense of calm. I realized that there was *nothing* he could do to keep me, short of building a cage.

I started to make plans and whisper them to my brother. The "Dive and ROLL" never materialized because we couldn't find the right time to open the door and JUMP.

I had one plan that I was confident would work. My brother and I had friends in my father's town. We would escape to our friends' houses and get bus money from their mothers. We'd be home in a day.

plan B.

But then, about
3 hours into the
drive, my father suddenly
turned the car around and
drove us back home. He never
said anything, he just dropped
us at the corner and we ran
in the back door to our mom.

This experience changed me completely. I realized that I didn't have to accept an outcome that I did not want, that was within my means to change. I discovered that I was resourceful; I had a way out. I was not trapped and I knew I could take care of myself.

DRIVE Q&A

WHY DO YOU THINK YOU WERE ABLE TO BE SO CALM AND LEVELHEADED IN THAT SITUATION?

I have often thought about that and struggle with defining the reason why. Immediately after the incident I was petrified to be alone in the house— I was frozen in fear, always watching the door. It took me a long time to feel safe alone with a man in a car .

Overall I think it has to do with the fact that I have a strong gut instinct and this somehow made me feel confident in a very scary situation. This is a skill I have carried through life in terms of problem solving: taking chances, trusting my gut, identifying solutions.

It also had to do with my brother. That drive changed the nature of our relationship; I stopped depending on him as my big brother. I had to take charge and take care of him. He wanted my dad's approval so badly he could never stand up to him. I needed that approval less because I had such a good relationship with my mom.

HOW DID THAT EXPERIENCE AFFECT YOUR RELATIONSHIP WITH YOUR FATHER?

During my first visit with him two years later, I was terrified he would trap me, cage me in the house to keep me. I hardly slept during that visit, and for years after I struggled with feeling guilty for not trusting him. I kept trying to establish a relationship between us—I'd arrange family get-togethers, I even moved in with him for a while—but in the end, the effort was all mine. He kept disappointing me, and I kept feeling responsible.

Finally, with the help of a counselor, I realized that I had the right to say goodbye to him for good, to not feel guilty about it, and to not feel I owed him something just because I was his daughter.

I was **eleven** when my family moved to Canada. My parents separated soon after, and my father was no longer in the picture.

We moved into a mostly white neighborhood, and from the second I walked into my new school I knew I was different. I felt confused over the fascination the other students had with me.

macaroni
tuesday

As I grew older
I became hyper-aware
of the little ways
I didn't Fit in.

My first real
Boyfriend was White
and came from a very
conservative and Wealthy
family. We went to a dinner
party at his house where I
quickly realized I was the
only person of color in the
room. I nervously answered
a barrage of questions: What
was my "Background," how
long had I lived here, what
did my parents do?

she's so
exotic!

They were all
shocked when I told them
my mother was a scientist.
Why was this so impressive?
They were all
Doctors or Engineers or
Judges. Was it because
she wasn't White?
I was so angry. I quietly
excused myself, walked
straight to the bathroom,
and burst into tears.

All I could think about was what my future would be like. I felt as though I had been put on trial in order to get a stamp of approval. I realized at that party that I wasn't just "different" anymore; I would never belong.

EXOTIC Q&A

WHY DID IT BOTHER YOU SO MUCH THAT PEOPLE SAW YOU AS EXOTIC OR DIFFERENT?

Being viewed as exotic totally displaced me; I didn't know where I belonged or how to fit in. I had never felt that way before. After I arrived in this country, I never felt as though I was treated as anyone's equal; everything I did or achieved was judged in light of my "difference."

Pretty soon I realized that I no longer fit in to my own culture either. My views, my mannerisms, and my appearance were drastically different from the traditional expectations of my community. This made me feel even more different and displaced.

No one ever asked me if I even wanted to come here. I was never given a choice; I was simply taken from one place and planted in another, and now that I'm old enough and have a choice, I belong to neither.

IS THERE ANYTHING THAT HAS HELPED TO EASE YOUR SENSE OF DISPLACEMENT?

It stayed with me for a long time. As I grew older I learned that I was not the only one who felt this way; there were so many others just like me, lost between two cultures. Growing up in a white community, I didn't meet all these other displaced souls. When I went to university I met many.

Now I try to look at my sense of displacement as an advantage. I'm aware of the flaws in both cultures; not feeling particularly connected to one or the other allows me to have my own opinions and not be swayed by a sense of belonging or duty. I'm not really ever bound to one place or one culture. Thinking about it in that way makes me feel incredibly free.

One night, when I was 13. I sat down to dinner with my mom, dad, and younger brother. My brother and I liked to joke around, and sitting across from each other we would try to get in a few kicks. My brother was a suck artist and would sometimes whine and pretend to be hurt. Most times we would laugh about it later. But not always, especially if dad was in a bad mood.

What did you do?

I just sat there with my nose bleeding, dripping into my mashed potatoes. my mother and brother were stunned, and silent.

My nose ached
but I didn't touch it.
I got up and walked to
the bathroom, letting
warm blood spill
down my shirt and
onto the floor.

BASTARD!
i'll never hit
my kids.
Such an
asshole
I Hate him

That one punch
set me on a course of
separating my identity
from my father's. I simply
realized I didn't want to
be like him. Not that I
knew who I wanted to be
like. But I was certain,
right then, it was not him.

PUNCHED Q&A

HOW DID YOU COPE WITH THE INCIDENT AFTER IT HAPPENED?

I was blown away and I didn't know how to make sense of it. I knew I hadn't done anything so wrong as to deserve that. My father came into my room about an hour later. He put his hand on my back and asked me if I wanted to watch the football game. I wanted to make him suffer so I ignored him; it was the only power I had.

I didn't talk to anyone about it because I was embarrassed, embarrassed for my father. I tried to forgive him but couldn't, so I buried it. Nobody wanted to believe it had happened so we just pretended it never did. It passed without anyone saying much.

HOW DID THAT EXPERIENCE SHAPE YOUR IDENTITY IN THE LONG RUN?

There had been other issues with my father but somehow that incident was the breaking point for me. It snapped me into a place where I had to find a way to deal with it.

There was an assumption that I would go into the family business. I started to think about my future and realized that I had to make some choices so I wouldn't end up like my father. I worked really hard in school so I would have other options. I wanted to go somewhere else, be someone else.

I started to look for places where I could escape my anger and sadness. As I got older, traveling allowed me to do this. It opened my mind to new things and new people.

At times, I have seen my father's temper in myself, and I have been able to catch it before it gets destructive. A specific part of my identity relies on not forgetting what happened to me as a kid. I think because of this I have a lot of empathy and patience for people who have experienced violence and abuse.

In high school, my friends and I went to concerts at a club that was in a pretty rough neigborhood. We were underage and we lied to our parents about where we were going. We had become so relaxed about being there that we didn't think twice about the kind of trouble we could get into.

Oh yeah, we come here all the time.

One night, as usual, we had gotten Quite drunk, and had smoked some pot. When we left the club we weren't paying attention to our surroundings. After walking about 6 blocks back to the subway, we finally noticed that a group of older guys was following us.

5 v3

We had no idea what to do so we confronted them. We were all pretty cocky and not one of us stopped to think about how this situation could get out of hand. My friend Ray started yelling at them, daring them to do something.

They charged and began
attacking us. For about 45
seconds it was total chaos,
fists and bodies were flying.
everywhere. There were
five of us and 8 of them.
We completely got our
asses kicked.

"Most of us managed to get away after a few blows. Just as I was about to make a break for it, I saw Ray face down on the sidewalk. He'd been robbed and was bleeding from his nose and arm, but they wouldn't stop beating him because he was still shouting at them with all of his might.

I knew I had to do something
so I ran over and tried to
drag him out of the situation.
Just then our friends returned
with a cop and the guys who
jumped us scattered.

"That was the first time that I really had to face the fact that my stupid actions can have very dangerous consequences. After that night, I never let myself get into such a compromising situation again.

THE FIGHT Q&A

WHAT WAS IT THAT MADE YOU GUYS SO COCKY IN THAT SITUATION?

We were 16 years old and wasted after the show; we felt invincible. As far as we were concerned we were the only people in the city that night.

Nothing negative had happened to us up to that point, except for running from cops a couple of times, so we never imagined the real trouble we could get into. That fight was enough to make us realize that change was necessary; we couldn't just go around behaving like we ruled the world anymore. It was a cold slap of reality and we all quickly (and painfully) became aware of how our behavior could get us in trouble, and even get someone really hurt.

HOW DID THAT NIGHT AFFECT YOUR FRIENDSHIP WITH THE GUYS YOU WERE WITH?

Afterwards, the cop dropped us off at Ray's house and his mother gave us an earful about it. But it really didn't matter; we were so relieved to be inside and safe that she could have said just about anything to us.

It was a pretty defining moment for us, individually and collectively. We talk about it all the time and joke about it now, but we all remember it clearly and have changed as a result. In some ways, I think that incident kind of bonded us for life. We helped each other that night, and we've helped each other make smarter decisions since.

MOM

My mother was not like those perfect mothers I saw on TV. ALL she did was sleep, read, and hide on the couch. I lived in fear that someone I knew from class, or maybe a friend, would come to the door and see what my home was like.

fly str

make some tea.

When I was 10, I became
what I thought a mother was
supposed to be. I learned
how to cook and take care
of my sisters so that no one
would find out how angry
and sad my home really was.

We weren't rich but for some reason my parents pretended that we were. I took piano lessons, dance lessons, and had a fancy leather jacket, but there was no food in the house and I often didn't have enough money to take the bus to school.

The day I turned 16
I went out and got my
driver's license. My father
was a mechanic and for my
birthday he built me a car. He
went to the junkyard and found
the body of a sports car that
had been in an accident. He
fixed it up, put in an engine,
and painted it blue. It was
beautiful.

I thought that car
would give me freedom. Instead
it tied me even more to
the responsibility of taking
care of my family.

to do

- go to bank
- Groceries
- take sie to dance
- deal with bathroom!
- Everyone to youth Group.

Even though I was
disappointed with my
mom for not being
there for me, I grew
up with a strong sense
of myself and my ability
to take care of things.

MOM Q&A

HOW DID HAVING ALL THAT RESPONSIBILITY AS A KID SHAPE YOU?

I like to be in charge and I know that this comes from my experiences growing up. Things were so chaotic and unpredictable in my house. By taking control and caring for everyone I found a way to feel calmer about it all.

As a teenager I was not very confident and I was lonely. I didn't really think I deserved friends. I thought I had to do things for people, often at my own expense, so that they would accept me. (Like chauffeur people around in that car!) Thinking back, I probably also did things for people, for my family, so that they would depend on me and not leave me.

One important thing that helped to ease my loneliness was the cultural youth group I belonged to. There I did have some friends and felt less like an outsider. We would spend six weeks together every summer at camp. It was a place I could just be "me."

IF YOU HAD THE CHANCE TO DO IT ALL OVER AGAIN, WOULD YOU DO IT ANY DIFFERENTLY?

I didn't get to experience the freedom, particularly the freedom from being responsible for other people, that I think childhood should bring. I wish I didn't have to grow up so quickly. If I could go back, maybe I would learn how to take more time for me, to find more personal space, and to be selfish—just a little.

But I do believe that we are made up of the things we experience in life, of where we come from. My background has made me a good friend and a responsible person. I had to live that life in order to be who I am today.

STUCK

we'll have this!-
all cleared out soon!

When I was **11** years old my parents sent me to a new school. It had just been built next to the church where my dad was the parish priest.

this is a wonderful addition to our community

One day at recess a small group of us, including the son of the school principal, headed outside to sneak a cigarette. There were lots of places we could hide.

But we couldn't hide the smell of smoke that was all over us. The principal came running up behind us, grabbed me by the ear, and twisted it hard. He didn't say a word to his own son.

Your father is the **Priest!**
You must be Better than the Others

He was smoking too.

For a long time I struggled with my resentment toward my father — for being who he was, and causing me to be seen as a "freak, a "goody-two-shoes", and for making me be an example for the rest of the kids.

When I was 13 I rebelled against this image. I started to do stuff like steal a few ounces of booze from my parents' liquor cabinet to drink with friends under the railway bridge.

Then I started to smoke pot and read Hermann Hesse and Robert Heinlein.

I developed my own beliefs about the nature of good and evil, religion, and sexuality... all of which I kept carefully hidden from my parents.

The injustice of
being singled out because
of who my father was, and
all the implications of that
experience, stayed with me
for a long time. In the end,
my rebellion was a good
and necessary thing
because it let me be
the master of my
own identity.

STUCK Q&A

WHY WEREN'T YOU THE "MASTER OF YOUR OWN IDENTITY" BEFORE YOUR REBELLION?

For years, from the earliest I can remember, my parents would ask me what I wanted to be when I grew up and I would say, "A priest." It was like a party trick. By the time I was 11 or 12, I realized that was what my parents wanted me to be, but not what I wanted to be. It took me years to get up the courage to tell them that I was not going to be a priest. When I finally did, my mother would just say, "Well, you may change your mind."

That rebellion, trying all the things I knew they would hate, was a way for me to separate from them.

SO IT WAS ALL ABOUT GETTING AWAY FROM YOUR PARENTS?

Not completely. It was also about finding ways to connect with my friends. Instead of letting them focus on our differences, I downplayed who my father was and made my own choices.

My rebellion also allowed me to learn about myself outside of the context of my family. A really important part of that learning came from certain writers and books that spoke to me in a profound way, much more than the stories in the Bible that I was forced to read. I often felt like a "stranger" among my friends but these books made me feel like there was hope. They put into words how I felt but had never been able to vocalize. It was a powerful realization to discover that my beliefs, especially about something as paramount in my life as religion, were actually universal.

Ironically, as I got older I also developed an appreciation for some of the lessons my father had taught me, things like human kindness and trying not to judge others too harshly. I've never shared his unshakeable, unquestioning religious faith, but the resentment I felt toward him has totally melted away.

freefall

When I think about my adolescence, I think of myself in freefall. People always tell teenagers to "just be yourself" but that never made sense to me. I had no idea who I was, and I was constantly trying to be the person I thought I was SUPPoSed to be, with no success.

From an Outside perspective, I didn't look too badly off. I was bright and on the swim team, I wrote for the school paper, I had friends and a couple of boyfriends along the way; I was reasonably attractive, and my family lived in a safe, middle-class neighborhood.

But I was Miserable.
My parents were constantly
telling me that I was a terrible
disappointment to them and that I
needed to change myself completely,
or else they just ignored me.
I was always comparing myself to
other people and feeling like a
FAiLURe. I had an eating
disorder that took up LOTS
of my time and energy.
           I drank and took
drugs whenever I could. I Hated
myself and thought about Suicide
a lot.

In my senior year of
high school I became the
editor-in-chief of the
school paper. That job was
my only refuge. I was good
at it and the work was
really [self-contained.] The
office was a kind of escape from
everything else in my life.
I took great pride in the
paper and the night before
each issue came out, I
would stay up all night
reading, editing, and
rewriting every article.

Those solitary nights, absorbed in work at my desk, were the foundation for everything good that was ever going to come of me. They gave me the space I needed to finally start liking who I was and to dream about who I might become.

FREEFALL Q&A

WHAT WAS IT ABOUT LOSING YOURSELF IN YOUR WORK THAT YOU FOUND SO SATISFYING?

It was first and foremost a distraction, a relief from what was going on at home. Later I came to realize that by being successful at work (and eventually getting paid to do what I loved) I could start to take steps toward independence and a better life apart from my family.

HOW DID YOU HANDLE ALL THOSE DEEPLY NEGATIVE FEELINGS ABOUT YOURSELF, THE ONES THAT MADE YOU THINK ABOUT SUICIDE AND LED TO AN EATING DISORDER?

I don't know that I did handle them in the sense of getting them under control; they were pretty much constant. Things grew worse before they improved, and I still struggle in some ways.

But working on something that was meaningful to me, and building my competence in an area I cared about, was something I could do despite those negative thoughts and feelings. Writing worked for me because it also involved a lot of reading. This opened me up to new stories and experiences that gave me a sense of hope, as I learned that I wasn't alone in my despair about my life; other people were miserable too. I think that coming to see myself in the context of the big, complex world, rather than within the narrow confines in which I grew up, was very important.

After high school I spent a year in England, which meant getting away from my mother. This was a turning point for me. Away from her, I learned to care for myself; I stopped trying to become what I thought others expected me to be.

AFTERWORD

WHO AM I? WHERE DO I FIT IN?

These are questions we ask ourselves all our lives. Sometimes we feel sure of who we are, while other times it's less clear. Every time we think we might know the answer, the people we meet and the experiences we live change us.

How you answer these questions will shape the decisions you make, the paths you choose, and subsequently, the person you become. A strong identity will help you to answer them in the healthiest way possible. So it's important to make sure that the image you have of yourself is a positive one.

If your story involves people or events that are abusive, hurtful, or unreliable then you may find that you start to identify as someone who only bad things happen to. You may even label yourself as someone who doesn't deserve to be happy.

Labels are sticky and can be hard to shake. That's why labels, especially negative ones, can be so suffocating; they don't leave much room for change. By placing people in categories—losers, jocks, divas, nerds—we attempt to control and explain life in a tidy way. But life isn't tidy; it's actually quite messy.

And as a teenager your mess is under a microscope. You have adults watching you and telling you what you should or shouldn't be doing. You're living through the drama of high school, fueled by a world of social networking and instant messaging. This means you're probably dealing with a hotbed of labels, judgment, and daily inspection. All this pressure can make it pretty hard to figure out who you are and where you fit in.

WHY SHOULD I CARE?

Imagine that you start out as a clean slate and then get scribbled on as time goes by. Like a chalkboard, every time you erase that scribble a chalky residue remains—it lies underneath the next layer of scribble as a kind of under-padding. This is the foundation of your identity. So, while you can reinvent your-self, traces of who you have been remain and influence, even in the slightest of ways, who you will become.

WHAT CAN I DO?

There's no doubt that it can be hard to build a strong and positive identity, especially in a crazy world where you may not have the resources, supports, or opportunities to give you a lift. And you may not be able to make huge life changes right now, but you can start by making a commitment to yourself to think critically about who you are and to be open to change. This kind of thinking will build your resilience—and that is the greatest power of all.

Resilience is about finding your strengths and using them to identify positively with who you are. You likely already have some of the tools that can help you do this: humor, confidence, assertiveness, empathy, independence, social skills, good friends, a great mentor, or goals and aspirations. Being resilient means that you can roll with the punches and get back up when you're knocked down, no matter what your story.

Thinking about your own story may also get you thinking about the stories of other people in your life. This can give you a whole new perspective on your friends and family, one that can strengthen your relationships or help you end ones that are unhealthy.

We all know that there's no easy path in life, and there's no magic formula for success or happiness. The best way to prepare yourself is to really understand, and hopefully like, who you are. This way you can face the future head on, more confident about your ability to tackle the tough challenges and more likely to enjoy the good ones.

RESOURCES

As you continue to ask yourself "Who am I?" you might find the following resources helpful, or at least thought-provoking. There is no shortage of good books that address the issue of personal identity, so I have chosen a few that I hope will resonate with all readers. I have also included a list of websites that address specific issues you might be struggling with, and a few phone numbers that might come in handy if you're feeling like the stuff you're dealing with is overwhelming.

HOTLINES

You can call any of these numbers 24/7 if you need help right away or if you need advice or support on a specific issue. They all offer crisis intervention, information, and referrals to emergency, social service, and support resources. All calls are anonymous and confidential.

If you're not in a rush to connect with someone, most also offer online counseling through email or live chat, so check out their websites (it can take a few days to get a response from an online counselor).

Remember, if it's an emergency dial 911.

In **Canada** there is one national youth hotline that can help you deal with any issue. You will be connected with a counselor who will support you and can refer you to services in your community.

Kids Help Phone: 1-800-668-6868

In the **U.S.** there are several national hotlines that offer counseling, support, and local referrals.

Childhelp National Child Abuse Hotline: 1-800-422-4453
National Hopeline Network (suicide prevention): 1-800-442-4673
National Runaway Switchboard: 1-800-786-2929
National Sexual Assault Hotline: 1-800-656-4673
National Teen Dating Abuse Helpline: 1-866-331-9474
The Trevor Helpline (gay, lesbian, bisexual, and transgender youth): 1-866-488-7386

BOOKS

FICTION

Almost every book of teen fiction has some identity thread in it. Below is a short list of books featuring young characters trying to figure out who they are and where they fit in. Consider these as a starting point if you're not sure where to begin.

The Absolutely True Diary of a Part-Time Indian. Sherman Alexie. Little Brown
    Books for Young Readers, 2009.
Bronx Masquerade. Nikki Grimes. Speak, 2003.
Skim. Mariko Tamaki and Jillian Tamaki. Groundwood, 2008.
Speak. L. Anderson. FSG Kids, 1999.
Waiting for Normal. Leslie Conner. Katherine Tegen Books, 2008.

NON-FICTION

There are a lot of non-fiction books that address some of the bigger issues that can affect your identity, like depression, abuse, poverty, sexuality, and sex. Here are a few:

*The Courage to Be Yourself: True Stories by Teens about Cliques, Conflicts,
    and Overcoming Peer Pressure.* Al Desetta. Free Spirit Publishing Inc., 2005.
It's Complicated: The American Teenager. Robin Bowman. Umbrage Editions, 2007.
The Little Black Book for Girlz. St. Stephen's Community House. Annick Press, 2006.
The Little Black Book for Guys. St. Stephen's Community House. Annick Press, 2009.
*The Shared Heart: Portraits and Stories Celebrating Lesbian, Gay, and
    Bisexual Young People.* Adam Mastoon. HarperCollins Canada, 2001.
When Nothing Matters Anymore: A Survival Guide for Depressed Teens.
    Beverly Cobain. Free Spirit Publishing Inc., 2007.

There are some good online book lists that are regularly updated where you can find out more about these books and others that might interest you. Check out:

www.teenreads.com

Teen Reads: Part of The Book Report Network, this site has an Ultimate Reading List with brief descriptions of each book listed.

www.ala.org/yalsa

The Young Adult Library Services Association: Part of the American Library Association, they have good book lists (and awards) like Quick Picks for the Reluctant Reader and Teen Top Ten.

WEBSITES

Websites are great because they are easy to update and to keep relevant. Plus, they can offer interactive features that can help you dig deeper into a subject. Not all websites are supportive though, so beware of sites that promote harmful behaviors, like cutting and eating disorders.

GENERAL
www.kidshelpphone.ca
This is the website of Kids Help Phone, Canada's national youth hotline. The **Get Informed** section covers a variety of issues and links to other resources for more information.

www.kidshealth.org
Produced by Nemours, a non-profit health organization, this website is full of friendly and non-judgmental information on issues affecting your physical and emotional health. Click on the **Teens** section to find the answers to all the questions you were too afraid to ask out loud.

MENTAL HEALTH
www.mindyourmind.ca
An award-winning site for youth by youth, this is a place where you can get information, resources, and tools to help you manage stress, crises, and mental health problems. Check out the interactive features in the **Mind Tools** section.

www.copecaredeal.org
This is a mental health site for teens. It's divided into three sections: **COPE** (tips on coping), **CARE** (ways to take care of yourself), and **DEAL** (information on mental illness).

SEX & SEXUALITY
www.sexetc.org
The website of Sex, Etc., part of the National Teen-to-Teen Sexuality Education Project developed by the Network for Family Life Education at Rutgers University. It is designed by teens for teens, and has tons of information on sexual health.

www.teenwire.com
The website of Planned Parenthood Federation of America, containing lots of information on healthy sexuality.

VIOLENCE
www.loveisrespect.org
This site has important information on dating abuse—from what it is, to how and where to get help. It's part of the National Teen Dating Abuse Helpline.

www.breakthecycle.org
The goal of this website is to educate and empower youth about domestic violence. It also links to its project site on dating violence (**www.thesafespace.org**), which includes a graphic novel and other dating violence resources and information.